I0830507

DIFFERENT

KINDS OF

PEOPLE

(Know who you are dealing with and how to deal with them)

Alexander Copland

To all the people in the world who have
remained strong despite character-altering
threats

TABLE OF CONTENTS

INTRODUCTION

In this book, you will be introduced to different kind of people who you will likely meet in office, your street or anywhere at all. It is necessary you know about them so that you guard against their negative attributes and also appreciate their good sides.

Nobody is permanently set to become one of them. People can change. Nurture can even affect that which is known to be nature. The pained and vindictive person could someday become the cheerful and free-minded kind and vice versa. As people live their lives, they begin to adjust based on how their experiences affect them. So, don't assume that someone will always be a certain way forever.

Learn about these different kind of people and also ensure you're not trapped into

become any of the kind that you consider
undesirable. Happy reading!

CHAPTER ONE

DIFFERENT KINDS OF PEOPLE IN THE WORKPLACE

The realist

The realist is glued to things that can be observed. They confront life on the basis of past experiences. They do not like building castles in the air. They are more paranoid and more careful when it comes to applying ideas that can't see their practicality. Reality is their drug. They want to relate what is to what has been. Realists channel their energy into practical problem-solving as against winning an argument or the mere successful postulation of a theory. They prefer ideas that has direct link with solving human problems. Many realists end up as engineers, policemen, carpenter, architects and so on.

The Investigator

He is interested in research. He is preoccupied with gathering of data, organizing data, analysing data, acquiring new knowledge, creating systems and solving complications in the abstract realm. He loves learning new theories, discovering new things in sciences and so on. They are the curious kind. Many of them enjoy being research fellows, lecturers, scientists, mathematicians, physicists, etc.

The Artist/Artiste

The artiste loves self-expression. He delights in trying out things for himself. He loves reading, dancing, drawing, singing, performing musical instruments, attending book fairs, practicing yoga, painting, acting etc. He loves natural things that engages motion and creativity. He loves cooking and traveling. He focuses on creativity, passion, independence and being open-minded. He places a high value on aesthetics. We find him becoming a singer, painter, dancer, photographer, actor, sculptor, writer, chef etc.

The Socialite

This kind of people concentrate on meeting people, building relationships, working together with others, helping others, inter-personal communication, interaction, collaboration, group work and volunteering. for something. They tend to talk too much. They are humanistic and cooperates well with others. Many people under this category are therapists, caregivers, teachers, counsellors and so on.

Enterpriser

They love taking risks, trying new things, proving ideas, public speaking, competitive activities, money making ventures, arguing ideas, managing people in a firm and so on. They are full of energy and ambition. They possess leadership attributes and are very competitive. Enterprisers are usually entrepreneurs, politicians, Human/Public Relations officer, human resource managers, public speakers, investors, salespersons and so on.

Conventionalists

This kind loves working with data of various kinds. They play attention to details. They love using computer a lot. They love filing and organizing information appropriately. They enjoy making calculations about facts. They are also deeply concerned about following procedures at working places. They detest going against the rules and delving wildly into new things. They are too concerned about being accurate and precise. They find it easier to follow things that are structured opposed to a scattered system.

They are usually very respectful. They always focus on efficiency and effectiveness. They do not want to waste time and energy on things that won't yield results. This kind enjoy being accountants, librarians, bankers, administrators and so on.

CHAPTER TWO

DIFFERENT KINDS OF PEOPLE ON THE STREET

Manipulative people

These are people who concentrate on getting what they want from you using deceitful means. They would act like they are friends but in reality, they are spies. They do everything possible to gain your approval, trust and respect. Just when you think you've got a trusted friend, they will hit you unprepared. They use several manipulative skills like loud generosity, friendliness and closeness, making you believe they can be trusted by offering to help all the time etc. They prey on simple-minded people who would not easily detect their tactics. The simple people easily take their generosity for kindness and thereafter open the doors of their lives to them.

Once the manipulator gains access, he identifies various things that characterizes the life of his prey. He studies his emotions, weaknesses, strength and close friends. Armed with this, he maps out strategies on how make him to do his bidding. With each success, they take a higher plan.

Manipulators also use pity-plan. The pity-pan is a strategy to appear like they need help just to get what they want from you. Out of pity, the prey succumbs. They can do a lot of things to appear pity-worthy. Many of do not stop when they get little. They go for more until the prey gets emptied and they disappear out of sight. Manipulative people make lots of plans. They ensure that their sources of information do not leak out.

Manipulative people do not always use the pity-plan. They also use the boss plan. It could be the use of 'age factor', or 'more knowledgeable' figure, 'more gifted' figure and so on. What they do is to make themselves appear larger than you so that you will trust and heed their advice or take their opinion without much questions. They may constantly remind you how they are older than you, more schooled than you, more exposed or travelled than you, more talented than you and all that. The idea is to get you to leave out your opinions. The goal of everything is to get something from you, get you to do something against your natural wish or get you to react in a particular way under a particular circumstance.

Sometimes, people manipulate in group. They plan how to devour their prey and appear one by one to carry out their strategies. You may never know that all of them are of the same group. They come with different patterns. This method is usually applied when what is to be gained is large or the person involved is too tough or there is more than one person to be manipulated. Manipulators can become forceful or firm when they have gained a great deal of control. They use this trick when it appears you are beginning to realize yourself. They can even go as far as threatening you if you don't comply. They block all the possible routes of escape ahead of time. They severe you from potential sources of help and make everything about you revolve around them. Manipulative people do not like obeying authorities. Their ability to manipulate other people give them a false sense of power and superiority. Besides, they do not want the chains of power to cut across their structures of manipulation.

How to deal with manipulators: Sometimes the simple-hearted while trying to get away from this kind, goes into negotiation. You do not negotiate with them. They are very smart. If you want them to go, cut them off totally by all means. Do not listen to their manipulative pleas. They can even send people to you to plead so they can have access to your life again. Do not consent! Ignore all the baits they use to get you, all of them. Their power lies in the various baits, pity and sense of superiority they've built over time. Make them know you no longer need their wisdom and protection.

Insecure people

These persons develop trait out of bad experiences. Sometimes, it comes as a natural trait. People who are insecure act in defence even when it is not necessary. In doing this they overdo things. They not trust anyone and spend so much time, energy and resources building walls of safety and setting boundaries. Because they never feel safe, they are always on the vigilant mode. It is hard to convince this kind of people that you are harmless. Sometimes, their defence makes them descend into deep selfishness. They do not believe that someone would possibly care about them. They even see your caring and gifts as a bait they must avoid. Many of them are past victims of manipulators. They can go any length to offend anyone so long as they feel it is for the purpose of self-preservation. For this reason, they do not usually have friends or much friends.

The insecure man could be planning revenge against you for a perceived wrong done against him even when you are not yet aware they are feeling you wronged them. They would exchange warm pleasantries with you while devising evil against you.

They exploit their closeness with you to know exactly how to come in with their plans. They do not always confront their perceived aggressor because they are not even ready to believe their side of the story. Also, being fearful people, they do not confront easily. Attacking from behind appears more comfortable for them. If you are close to them, they want to put up strict measure that will ensure you do not betray them. This could make them become harsh, stern and unnecessarily principled towards you. They amplify the good they do for you as a reminder that they are not worthy of betrayal.

How to deal with insecure people: Do not allow them into your space and when they are around you do not be free with them. Scold them when necessary and be stern with them. They are usually afraid of bold moves. Do not make them see you as weak.

Pained/Angry/Vindictive people

This kind transfer aggression from one person to another. They are never divorced with their past. They view everything from the eyes of revenge. This type can plan a revenge mission for a very long period of time. Their hurt becomes the motivating force of their lives. For this kind, partial revenge is not enough. They don't stop until they feel they have done enough. They can be patient for however long it takes to revenge. Pained people never give trust a second chance. For some of them, they withdraw into their shell of inactivity. Their fear of being hurt again makes them reduce activities that involve others, especially the one that caused the pain. Pained and vindictive people are hardy happy. There is always something hurting them. They are more sensitive to pain than the average person around them. They tell everyone that care to listen about the hurt and the offender as a way appearing as the innocent and aggrieved person. By this, they try to draw others into their game of vindication. If they get enough persons, they form a gang of vengeance. This kind of group activity gives them joy as they assume its leadership being the first to start it up. They try to help others see that they should be hurting too. They emphasise and point out the wrong of others towards them as vividly as possible. In their misery, they love company.

How to deal with the pained and vindictive: Leave their group immediately if you've been trapped in one. Refuse to grant them audience thenceforth. Also, distant yourself from the people who are with them. Beware of them for you could be a target. Remember they pick offence just from anything including a perceived bad eye look. You will never know that an innocent eye look is attracting hatred and revenge to you. Try to notice when thoughts come to you in the fashion of their mind set and discard them immediately. Exiting their group doesn't not mean that the seeds they have planted in you will die overnight. Keep uprooting them till no trace is left. Remember, having dismembered from them, you could be a point of attack. Beware!

Cheerful, carefree, free minded people

This kind of people are open. They do not first assume someone out there is out to hurt them. They start out with trusting people. They leave their lives open to people.

They are always happy, cheerful and accommodating. Their easy-going life earn them so many friends. It appears like everyone is their friend. They easily flow in and out of circles. They are also liberal people.

They relate with people with ease, learn new languages easily and get used to a new environment quickly. When they make entrance into an environment, everyone easily identifies them. They are usually loud and social people. They also found around feasts, parties, ceremonies etc. that is if they are not the ones organizing them. They are usually fun to be with as they are the kind that tell lots of stories, hold the latest news or gossip and are sometimes good in offering jokes. They are always full of laughter and fun

Mind you, this kind can be unreliable as they usually try to please everyone. They do not commit themselves to people. They've got no permanent friend nor permanent enemy. They easily shed crocodile tears to attract pity. They use the tool of their popularity to gain support to do whatever they want.

How to deal with the cheerful, carefree and free-minded: Do not gain from their activities. Stay away from them. This they will easily notice as it is usually few persons that are not in their flow. Do not rely on them for anything, for they are unreliable.

Strict, stern, principled people, goal-driven people

These are people who are driven by the need for achievements. They are so concerned with the need for achievement that they drive people so hard. For them, nothing matters more than their goals. They set standard for themselves and do not flinch despite life's vicissitudes. They drive people who work with them or around them to focus on the goal and nothing else. This gives them leadership drive to carry others along.

Some persons do find their standard too high or even unnecessary to keep. This attracts disputes and disagreements to them. They are usually strong enough to handle opposition. This gives them labels such as 'heady', 'non-conformist', 'tyrant', 'oppressor', 'wicked', 'inconsiderate' and so on.

People of this kind always stick to their words even when it hurts and expect others to do so. They look up to nothing less than perfection. Sometimes, this method earns them success, sometimes it doesn't. They have times when their followers argue with them about highhandedness. This people are not afraid to stand alone.

How to deal with the strict, stern, principled people, goal-driven people.

First of all, realize that this people are logical in nature. Do not engage them in a logical battle. Rather win them with results.

The only thing they bow to is results. Do not oppose them in emptiness. Find ways to prove your points through achievements. Where you can't find achievements, get other to stand by you. They usually have so many enemies. In this case, their strong character becomes their defence while your company becomes your defence. Even at that, don't remove your eyes from the quest for results. Avoid trying to buy them over to your side. It gives them the feeling that you are weak and they will be more willing to strike you. Also ensure that you do not benefit from them. I can assure you that those benefits are better named baits to keep you on their side. People who are on their side cannot have opinion or contradiction. They derive pleasure in speaking for other people. Don't join their camp unless you are seeking their protection, and that at the cost of your freedom.

Religious/pious, spiritual people

These people are very much like the principled people. The only difference is that they practice what they do within the ambit of religion.

Religious people consider conformity to religion superior to human fleshly desires except in religions where humanity is put first. But you have to understand that religion must have a spiritual underpinning. This means that you can't practice religion at a human plane. This makes religion incompatible with human estate. For one to be spiritual, he or she has to transcend his or her natural state. Being spiritual requires a lot of discipline which include times of meditations, prayers, studying, attending necessary meetings.

All these point to the fact that a deeply religious person will not interact with you the same way a normal person would. He may have taboos, restrictions and limitations that will affect the way he relates with you and/or the way you relate with him. Pious people obey lots of spiritual laws and commandments. This should guide you in relating with them.

How to deal with religious, pious and spiritual people: You will need to know what their religion is as we as the restrictions. Religious persons are not bad or difficult people. You just need to know from them what constitute their spirituality and relate with them thus. In the case where you can't cope with their life, quit the relationship.

The Introvert and the extrovert

The introvert is withdrawn into himself. He enjoys spending more his time alone. He does not want to be bothered by the presence of too many people or their activities. He doesn't like attracting too much attention to himself. He takes time to think before he acts. He thinks right in his head as opposed to thinking out loud. He keeps friendship with few trusted persons. He prefers to listen than to talk while the extrovert is the exact opposite.

CONCLUSION

Having been exposed to different kinds of people and how to deal with them, remain armed against their negative sides. Also, use this as a guide against appearing as any of them who possess undesirable traits. Some of them are not necessarily bad people. They are people under the influence of nature or experiences. Some of them can still change from one kind to another. If you are careful enough with yourself, you can offer yourself as instrument of such change.

Visit www.amazon.com/authour/luckyeluemebooks for more books by the author.

OTHER BOOKS BY AUTHOR

What's stopping you?

The Sacrifice of Choice

Own the box, don't think out of the box

Best Ways to Retain Memory

Easy steps to Quality decision making

Finding true pleasure in marriage

Handing Imperfections

Goodbye depression

The Messi and the Ronaldo (the two kinds of winners)

Who am I?

What career fits me best?

And others

www.ingramcontent.com/pod-product-compliance
Lightning Source LLC
Chambersburg PA
CBHW061610250726
48657CB00017B/2410